NINE MICMAC LEGENDS

NINE MICMAC LEGENDS

by

Alden Nowlan

ILLUSTRATED

by Shirley Bear

LANCELOT PRESS

Hantsport, Nova Scotia

ISBN 0-88999-196-0

Published 1983

Second printing 1984

LANCELOT PRESS LIMITED, Hantsport, N.S.

Office and plant situated on Highway No. 1, ½ mile east of Hantsport

For Claudine and Johnnie
and to Aida Flemming
with love.

ACKNOWLEDGEMENTS

Five of the stories in this collection were previously published in *The Atlantic Advocate.* One of the five, "The Snow Vampire," appeared in *Toboggans and Turtlenecks*; another, "Three Boys and the Giants," appeared in *Hockey Cards and Hopscotch*; both books were edited by John McInnes and Emily Hearn, and published by Thomas Nelson and Sons (Canada), Ltd.

CONTENTS

INTRODUCTION

Every surviving Micmac legend, including the nine stories in this book, owes its continued existence to Rev. Silas T. Rand, who was for forty years a Baptist missionary among the Micmacs of Nova Scotia. Rand translated the Bible into Micmac and compiled a 40,000-word Micmac dictionary. He also gathered together a wealth of material about the *sakawachkik*, the people who are gone. Without Silas Rand, we might never have heard of Glooskap.

Born at Cornwallis, N.S., in 1810, Rand was a first cousin of Sir Charles Tupper, sixth Prime Minister of Canada. However, his only formal education, apart from a few months in a one-room country school where, according to his own account, the teacher could scarcely read and write, consisted of four weeks at Horton Academy in Wolfville, N.S., studying Latin grammar. At the age of 18 he took up his father's trade and became a bricklayer. Yet before he died in 1889, he taught himself 12 languages, including Micmac, Maliseet and Mohawk.

Like Britain's Prime Minister Gladstone, Rand amused himself by translating popular English hymns into Latin. Gladstone admitted that Rand's Latin version of "Rock of Ages" was "more exact" than his own.

Ordained to the ministry in 1834, Rand ministered to churches in Parrsboro, Horton, Liverpool and Windsor in Nova Scotia, and in Charlottetown, P.E.I., before becoming a missionary to the Indians. From 1853 until his death, he lived at Hantsport, N.S.

"I never found an Indian who would undertake to tell one of these stories in English," he wrote in the Introduction to a collection of his Micmac legends published by Longmans, Green and Company of New York in 1894.

A copy of that collection, long out of print and now obtainable only through rare book dealers, was lent to me by my friend, Mrs. Hugh John Flemming. I did the adaptations in the summer and fall of 1966, chiefly as a means of distracting myself while recovering from a serious illness.

In an oral culture, a story-teller feels free to relate a folk tale in his own way so long as he is true to the plot and spirit of the tale as it was told to him. I have granted myself the same liberty. This does not pretend to be a scholarly work. But I have been reasonably faithful, I think, to Rand and his Micmac sources. My deletions have consisted largely of references to birds, animals and what-not which the Ellenu (the name the Micmacs give themselves) could not have known about before the arrival of the first Europeans. Even so, the stories doubtless show a strong European influence. In Rand's time, the Micmacs had already been in touch with European culture for something like 250 years.

It ought to be borne in mind that these legends were not intended to be children's stories (although two of the nine in the present collection have appeared in books for children). They were stories told by an adult to other adults — the nearest a people without a written language could come to creating a literature.

Alden Nowlan

THE STAR BRIDES

In the days of the people who are gone, two beautiful young sisters were overtaken by night in the woods.

Knowing they could not hope to return to their village before daylight, they made themselves beds of pine boughs and lay down under the open sky, huddling together for warmth.

As they waited for the coming of sleep, they talked, as young girls will, of the young men they might one day marry.

The sky was cloudless and the stars were very bright. Sleep was slow in coming and the sisters were a little afraid. To comfort one another, they pretended the stars were the eyes of lovers, looking down at them protectively.

"I will choose that one to be my husband," said the elder sister, pointing at the sky. "His eyes are as bright as those of a hawk."

"And I will choose that one," said the younger sister, gesturing drowsily, "his eyes are as bright as those of an eagle."

The sisters laughed, fell silent and drifted off to sleep.

Then it was morning. Even before opening her eyes, the elder sister stretched her beautiful arms and legs.

"Be careful!" cried a voice, "you will spill my warpaint!"

Suddenly, the sisters were fully awake. They sat up quickly, their eyes wide with wonderment.

Here were two handsome young warriors. One, with eyes like those of a hawk, leaned on his spear. The other, with eyes like those of an eagle, knelt on the ground to mix his red warpaint.

Perhaps it was in that first instant of awakening that the sisters fell in love. Perhaps it took many days. Perhaps they only imagined that they were in love. In any event, it was not long before they were married: the elder sister to the warrior with the eyes of a hawk; the younger to the warrior with the eyes of an eagle.

For a time, they were happy. While their husbands hunted in the woods, the sisters cared for their wigwams.

But soon the sisters grew sulky because, near the wigwams, there was a large, flat stone which their husbands had strictly forbidden them to touch or move.

If their interest had not been aroused by their husbands' prohibition, the sisters might never have thought of touching the stone. As it was, they could not rest until their curiosity was satisfied.

So one day when the men were hunting for bear, the sisters pried up the stone and peered under it.

What they saw made them start back and cry out with fear. For the stone was like a trapdoor in the roof of the world.

Far, far below they saw the village of their childhood, surrounded by the forest in which they had fallen asleep.

"Our husbands are not men!" cried the elder sister.

"They are wizards!" cried the younger.

"They are star creatures!"

"And they have taken us to their home above the sky!"

The sisters embraced one another and wept and when their husbands returned home they would not leave off weeping.

"Did you not choose us to be your husbands?" the hawk-eyed man demanded.

"Did you not summon us when you lay in the forest?" demanded the eagle-eyed man.

"That was only a game," wept the elder sister.

"All girls play such games," wept the younger.

"Then you wish to return to your world?" asked the hawk-eyed man.

"Yes. Oh, yes. Please," the sisters agreed.

"Then you are free to go," said the man with the eyes of

an eagle. “But you must follow our instructions.”

That night the sisters were told they must sleep together, and they were to cover their faces.

“In the morning you must not be in haste to uncover your faces,” the star men warned. “Wait until you hear a chickadee sing; and even then you must not open your eyes. Wait still longer until you hear the red squirrel sing; and still you must wait. Keep your faces covered and your eyes closed until you hear the striped squirrel sing. Then open your eyes and uncover your faces and you will be safe.”

The sisters sleep little that night and awoke early the following morning. They lay awake for a long time with their faces covered before they heard the singing of the chickadee.

The younger sister wanted to get up at once to see if they had in truth been returned to earth, but the elder sister restrained her.

“We must wait until the singing of the striped squirrel,” she reminded. “Be patient. We will soon be back in our own village.”

But when the red squirrel sang, the younger sister could control herself no longer. She uncovered her face and opened her eyes. And the moment she opened her eyes she found herself falling through the night — falling faster and faster toward the stoney floor of the world.

There was not even time for her to cry out, so her sister did not know she had disappeared until she heard the singing of the striped squirrel, uncovered her face, opened her eyes and found herself in the part of the forest where their adventures had begun.

However, as she looked up at the sky from which she had lately come, the elder sister saw a star falling through the gray of the early morning and knew that star was in fact her younger sister who had uncovered her eyes too soon and was doomed to fall forever toward the earth.

And to this very day when the people see a falling star they say it is the younger sister, still tumbling through the night.

There are even those who say that the morning star is

the hole in the sky through which the eagle-eyed warrior observes the eternal descent of his bride.

THREE BOYS AND THE GIANTS

In the days of the people who are gone, giants lived in the land, and hunted men, as men hunted animals.

One day a giant who was hunting for his dinner came upon three boys who had gone into the woods in search of partridge.

When the giant saw the children, his mouth began to water. He smacked his lips in anticipation of the feast that he and his brother would enjoy when he took this tender game back to his wigwam.

Quickly, he crouched down in a thicket where there was less danger that the children would see him, and considered how he might lure them deeper into the forest — for the village in which the children lived was nearby, and the giant knew if he struck too soon the cries of the children would summon their fathers who would drive him away and, perhaps, even kill him.

The giant thought for a long time before he hit upon an idea; for, fortunately for men, the minds of the giants were as weak as their bodies were strong — had this not been so, giants rather than men would now possess the land.

To the giant, his plan seemed the most cunning ruse that had been devised since the beginning of the world. He would imitate a partridge and, thus, decoy the boys into the deep forest where it would be safe to seize them. They would think they were about to obtain their game; in reality, the giant would be about to obtain his!

So the giant imitated the sound of the cock partridge by slapping his palms against his chest, and the three boys followed the sound, deeper and deeper into the woods.

At last, when he had lured them a great distance from their village, the giant burst out of the trees, seized the screaming children by their feet and dashed their heads against what he took to be a stone.

Luckily for the boys, it was not a stone but an anthill, so they were not killed but only stunned. But the giant was too stupid to realize this. Chuckling to himself, he dropped them, like so many partridges, into the birchen vessel which was strapped to his back.

"Ah! We will dine well tonight!" said he. "What juicy morsels the drumsticks of these little birds will make!"

And, walking very fast, he started off toward his wigwam.

He had not gone far when the boys awakened. The youngest would have cried out when he realized where they were, and where they were being taken, but the eldest put his hands upon his lips.

"Hush," he whispered, "if the giant discovers that we are alive he will wring our necks or crush our skulls. While he believes us dead, we have a chance of making our escape."

Now, the boys had dropped their bows and arrows on the ground when they were surprised by the giant; but the eldest carried a knife on a belt around his waist. With this knife, he cut a hole in the birchen vessel. One by one, as the giant strode through the forest, the boys slipped through the hole and dropped to the ground.

So strong was the giant that he was not aware that his load was becoming lighter and lighter. For the weight of a dozen children was as nothing to a giant who could uproot an oak as easily as he could pick up an acorn.

Even when the vessel was quite empty, the giant was not aware that his birds had flown. Only when he came to his wigwam and triumphantly invited his brother to examine the results of his day's hunting did he learn that he had been outwitted.

"You fool!" raged the brother. "We have nothing to eat

and our birchen vessel is ruined! If your meat were not so tough and my teeth were not so old and blunt, I would dine upon your own flesh! How dare you call yourself a hunter when even partridge chicks are more cunning than you!"

At first, the giants considered attempting to recapture the children. But, at last, since it was now beginning to be dusk, they resigned themselves to the loss of their dinner, and began to drowse beside the fire.

Meanwhile, the children had found their way back to the place where they had been attacked. Their bows and arrows still lay upon the ground.

The eldest boy gathered up his weapons.

"Now," he said, "we must find the giant and kill him."

"Don't be foolish," said the youngest boy, who longed for the warmth and safety of his father's wigwam. "We are too small and weak to kill a bear, let alone a giant. Only the greatest warriors dare challenge such creatures."

"The little one is right," said the third boy. "Let us go back to the village. Tomorrow, a war party will hunt down the giants."

"Would you bear children's names all your lives?" sneered the eldest boy. "Would you sit forever with your legs outstretched, as children sit in our wigwams? Or would you take men's names and sit cross-legged, as only men are permitted to do?"

The two younger boys fell silent, ashamed to confess to their fear. Rather than be branded cowards, they agreed to accompany the eldest boy to the wigwam of the giant.

Much later, the three, each with his bow in his hand and his quiver of arrows by his side, came to the place where the giants were encamped and lay down in the darkness, just beyond the circle of light created by the giants' campfire.

Now, it happened that the giants had not gone into their wigwam to sleep but had fallen asleep outdoors, beside the fire.

Taking careful aim, the eldest boy shot an arrow at the throat of the giant nearest him.

The arrow struck home but did not even awaken the giant, although he stirred in his sleep and scratched at the wound like one who had been bitten by a fly. The boy shot an arrow at the other giant, with the same result.

When his third arrow found its mark, the giant who was its target slapped at the spot where it had entered his flesh and muttered: "Those cursed mosquitoes!"

"Yes," agreed the other giant, who had been half-awakened by the boy's fourth arrow. "The nasty little bloodsuckers are biting hard tonight."

Soon, the younger boys screwed up sufficient courage to shoot at the giants.

Clouds of sharp shafts sank in the giants' bodies. The air was black with arrows as a swamp is black with flies.

"Ah!" mumbled one of the giants. "Those are not mosquitoes but hornets. Somebody must have disturbed their nest."

"Hornets or bees," growled the other.

The boys shot arrows at the giants until their quivers were almost empty. And every shaft found its mark.

"These are surely the largest hornets in the world," said the first giant.

"Bees, not hornets," said the other.

"Bees or hornets," said the first giant, "it makes no difference. They make sleep impossible. Let us go into the wigwam where they are less likely to disturb us."

The giants started to get to their feet, and the boys, hiding in the darkness, shivered with fear, for now their quivers were empty and at any moment the giants would realize what had happened and claim their revenge.

But, just as the boys prepared to throw down their now useless bows and run for their lives, the giants ceased struggling to stand up, fell back and lay still.

They were dead — killed without ever knowing they were being attacked.

The boys ran out of the darkness, into the light of the campfire and shouted and danced in the joy of their victory.

THE MAN WHO HATED WINTER

In the days of the people who are gone, there lived a great warrior who hated winter.

During the summer, this warrior was the happiest man in the village, but when winter came he was never seen to smile. Sometimes his anger was so great that he stood at the door of his wigwam and shook his fist in the face of the north wind, and often as he walked through the village he kicked at the snow as though it were the body of a treacherous enemy.

So great, in fact, was his hatred of cold and ice and snow that some believed that his spirit was possessed by those who fly through the air or that he had made some strange pact with those who whistle in the dark. But he was terrible in battle and a mighty hunter, so men feared him and let him live.

Now, at first the god of winter was amused by the warrior's antics. Once or twice he pinched the man's nose or ears with his icy fingers to make him even more furious. "Poor little man," he laughed, "he is like a rabbit who becomes enraged with a bear." But as time went on, the god began to lose his patience. When he came home to his wigwam after a hard day's work of scattering snow over the world, his wife would ask him what he had done that day to chasten the mortal who defied him. And when he would not answer her, she smiled to herself — one of those mocking feminine smiles that make even the gods uneasy.

When spring came and the ice broke up in the rivers and floated down to the sea, our warrior would not wait for the sun to melt the ice cakes left behind on the intervals. The people were amazed to see him attack the cakes with his war club, smash them to pieces and hurl the pieces into the river.

One day while the warrior was destroying the ice cakes, the god of winter determined to teach the unruly mortal a lesson he would never forget.

Seizing the largest ice cake he could find, the god hurled it at the mortal so that he was knocked into the icy river. Then, shouting his war cry, the god leapt into the water and closed his hands around his enemy's throat.

But, unhappily for the god, it was almost spring and his strength had begun to fail him. The warrior was able to break the god's grip and swim ashore, leaving the god so exhausted that had he not succeeded in climbing on a floating ice cake he might have drowned. And to add to his discomfiture as he floated away, the warrior stood on the bank and pelted him with ice and stones.

"Be off!" cried the warrior, "be off and never come back!" And the people of the village laughed to see their old adversary dance and tear his hair in rage as he sought to avoid the missiles hurled at him by the warrior.

And the warrior did not leave off pelting the god until the little island of ice on which he stood floated around a bend in the river and disappeared from sight.

The villagers did not laugh for long, however, for they knew that winter would not rest until he had his revenge. That night the people sat in council and decided the warrior who had humiliated the god should be banished from the village.

"Winter will return," the people reminded the warrior, "and when he returns he will surely kill you. If we allow you to remain among us, we and our children will also die."

So our rash warrior was sent off alone into the forest.

Summer came and it did not seem that it would ever end. While the sun smiled and the land was green, the warrior forgot his hatred of winter. Nor did he pine over his old village. He was content to wander alone through the forest and spend whole days lying in open places where the hands of the sun god caressed his body.

But when the leaves began to fall and there was need for a fire at night, he remembered the warning the villagers had given him. Yes, winter would return as he had always done — and this time he would attack in the fullness of his strength and there would be no limit to his rage.

"I will sell my life dearly," vowed the warrior. And he began to arm himself for the battle that lay ahead.

First, he built a wigwam bigger than any ever before seen upon the earth. Then he cut more logs than any man had ever cut before and split the logs into firewood and piled the firewood in his wigwam. He fashioned also a mighty bow and a great stack of arrows and a great axe with a handle of stone; and he killed moose and bear and brought their skins to his wigwam.

From the day when the first snow fell, he waited for the time when winter would come to exact his revenge. So he was not surprised when the day came that the god arrived and began to beat upon the walls of his wigwam.

"What, old fool! Would you have me trounce you a second time?" sneered the warrior. And he painted the sign of the sun god on his forehead, and the sign of the fire god on his cheeks and the sign of the lightning bird upon his chest — and did not forget to throw more wood on his fire.

Soon, the god, using his great war axe, succeeded in cutting a hole in the wall of the wigwam.

When he saw the god's face peering in through the hole the warrior put an arrow to his bow.

"Are you fool enough to think an arrow can wound me?" laughed the god. And his laughter was such that the wigwam shook, but the warrior was not afraid: before releasing his shaft he set fire to his arrow. Seeing this, the god ceased laughing and drew back from the hole in the wigwam. But he was not quite quick enough and the flaming arrow struck him in the shoulder.

"Now which of us is the fool?" demanded the warrior. And he smiled grimly as he heard winter rolling in the snow to heal the wound caused by the arrow.

If we were to tell all that happened during the battle that

followed, our tale would never end. It is said that for an entire season winter neglected the rest of the world, so intent was he on punishing the defiant warrior.

The god fought with javelins of ice and the man retaliated with his burning shafts.

Many times the god fought his way into the wigwam only to be driven back by the man's stone-handled axe, the blade of which he had left in the fire until it became red-hot.

Once, the god succeeded in stealing into the wigwam while the warrior slept, only to fall into a trap that sent him sprawling into the fire and all but killed him.

The warrior did not dare to leave his wigwam for fear the god would ambush him where there was no fire. But he did not starve — for the animals, who also hated winter, came to his wigwam willingly that he might eat them and live.

As the months passed, the adversaries grew weary. Both of them bore innumerable wounds. But as spring approached, the god was no more certain of victory then he had been when he felt the first of the warrior's flaming arrows.

One day he came to the door of the wigwam and told the warrior he wished to speak with him.

"We have fought long enough," he said. "I come to talk of peace."

"Come in, then," answered the warrior, "but be sure you are planning no tricks, for nothing would give me greater pleasure then to pierce your heart with a flaming arrow or cut off your head with my red-hot axe blade."

Winter entered the wigwam and seated himself as far as possible from the fire.

"Of course, I could kill you in time," said the god. "But I have other matters to occupy my attention. Do you know I no longer have time to freeze more than half the rivers in the world? Because of our quarrel many parts of the forest are bare of snow. My wife scolds me. My children complain that their friends tell them I am no more than half a god. My greatest rival, the god of summer, snickers behind my back."

The warrior began to feel a little pity for his old enemy.

"Your state is a sad one," he conceded. "But what would you have me do? Surely, you can't expect me to give up my life that you may maintain your pride?"

The god sighed and tried to move still farther away from the fire.

"I ask only that you cease to make men and gods laugh at me," said he.

"And I ask only that you leave me in peace," said the warrior.

So, at last, it was agreed between them. Never again did the warrior hold winter up to ridicule and never again did winter trouble the warrior. As long as the warrior lived — and it is said that he lived to be a very old man — he was never bothered by cold, ice or snow. It was never necessary for him to don warm robes or leggings. All year around he wore only a loincloth. And while all the rest of the world shivered in the grip of winter, the great warrior would lie on a green hillside in the bright sunlight and smell the flowers.

THE INVISIBLE BOY

In the days of the people who are gone, there lived a boy who was invisible, like the wind.

Even his parents could not see him. When he was a baby his mother could find him only by groping in the direction where she heard him crying.

When blankets were wrapped around the baby, they, too, became invisible. When his mother dressed him, the clothing disappeared. As he grew up it was discovered that a bow or spear vanished the moment he took it in his hand.

While still a child, he became a great warrior, for he could walk in broad daylight through the camp of the enemy without being seen. And, being invisible to beasts as well as to men, he became the greatest hunter his village had ever known: stealing upon the wiliest game and driving home his spear so unexpectedly the beast never knew whether it was man or lightning that struck it down.

One day a daughter was born to the parents of the invisible boy and to everyone's astonishment it was discovered that she was the only person in the world who possessed the power to see him. After their parents died, the brother and sister lived together in a large wigwam beside a beautiful lake.

Now, there were many unmarried girls in that country and any one of them would have been happy to have the invisible boy take her as his wife. After all, they reasoned, one who possessed such mysterious power must be favoured by the

gods: his wife was certain to bear sons who would do great deeds that would be recorded in the songs of the people. And the family of so mighty a warrior and hunter need never fear hunger, cold or the raids of the enemy.

Of course, they had no way of knowing whether he was handsome or ugly. But since they could not see him they were free to make pictures of him in their minds; and if a girl cannot see her husband's face, well, she can never tire of it, for if the face she has painted in her mind begins to bore her she has only to blink her eyes and it will be replaced by another.

But, alas, his sister insisted that his bride be able to see him. In fact, she promised that the first girl who proved that she could see him would become his wife. So every evening when he came home from the hunt girls would be waiting with his sister outside his wigwam.

"Ah! Here he comes now!" his sister would say. "Do you not see him? He is walking toward us, along the shore of the lake."

A few of the girls — a very few — would admit that they saw nothing. But most would look in the direction toward which the sister was pointing and exclaim: "Yes, yes, I see him! He is the handsomest of all the hunters and, as always when he returns from the hunt, his back is laden with meat."

At this, his sister would pretend to rejoice. She would embrace one of the girls who had spoken and address her as "sister."

"At last!" she would cry, "there is someone besides myself who can see him! How happy he will be! But tell me how he is dressed — I cannot remember what he wore when he left this morning and he is not yet close enough for me to make out his garments."

So cunning was the sister that the girls invaribly fell into her trap. They would tell her that his costume was like that of other young men of their village, except that it was richer or more beautiful. Or they would tell her that he wore the skins of animals no other man had ever slain. One might say he wore a jacket made from beaver pelts, another that he was clad in the skin of a white bear and wore the horns of a dragon upon his head. It did not matter. Either way, the sister would know that they were lying and would laugh at them and send them away.

Now, there lived in that village an old man, a widower, who had three daughters, the youngest of whom was puny and often sick. The two older girls considered the youngest a great nuisance and shamefully mistreated her: kicking and cuffing her about and burning her hands and face intentionally. When the father came in from the hunt and inquired about the bruises and burns on the girl's body, the older sisters would claim that she had run into a tree or fallen into the fire. "The gods have deprived the little one of her senses," they told him. "Or perhaps she is possessed of an evil spirit. She hurts herself in spite of everything we do to protect her." And they stared in mock pity at the girl, who cowered in the farthest corner of the wigwam, not daring to deny the truth of their words. The people called the girl Oochigeaskw which is translated: She Who Is Covered With Scars.

Both of the older girls had gone to wait for the invisible boy and both had fallen into his sister's trap and been sent home in disgrace.

"Did you see him?" asked Oochigeaskw timidly when they arrived home.

"Certainly, we saw him," they snarled. "But he was so ugly that we fled for fear that we would be made sick by the sight of his face. Why, he was almost as ugly as you!"

Then, as a pleasant way of passing a few idle moments, they each of them cut a stout birch switch and gave their youngest sister a sound thrashing; after which they amused themselves by cutting off her hair and throwing great handfulls of it into the fire. Soon they were enjoying themselves so much that they almost forgot their frustration at having been outwitted by the sister of the invisible boy.

But a fantastic thought had been planted in the mind of little Oochigeaskw. She had decided that she also would find out whether or not she possessed the power to see the invisible boy.

She dared not reveal her plan to her father: it would only have confirmed his belief that the gods had made her mad. But the next day she went to the wigwam where the boy lived with his sister.

She had clothed herself in a dress of birchbark and wore her father's moccasins because they were all she had to wear.

The people laughed at her as she walked through the village. How much harder they would have laughed if they had known her destination!

The girl might have lost her courage and turned back if the boy's sister had not come to meet her.

"Ah, little one," she said, "I perceive you are come to see if you are destined to be my brother's bride. Perchance, you may see him. But would you wish him to see *you* — disfigured with burns and scars and clad like one deprived of her wits?"

Oochigeaskw hung her head and would have slunk away, but the boy's sister took her by the arm and led her into the wigwam.

There she stripped her of her birchbark dress and ungainly moccasins and bathed her and massaged her body with oils so that all the scars and burns disappeared. Then she clothed her in a dress made from the skins of strange and beautiful beasts that the boy had killed; and she reached for a comb with which to comb her hair —

"Do not mock me," Oochigeaskw pleaded, "for you can see that my sisters have cut off my hair."

"Hush," replied the sister of the invisible boy. And, lo, under the touch of her comb the little one's hair grew long and beautiful.

"Now, let us go outside and watch for my brother for it is time for the men to return from the hunt."

The little one did as she was told and the two girls went outside and waited for the invisible boy.

Hardly an instant had passed when Oochigeaskw cried: "I see him! He is coming!"

"And how is he clad?" asked his sister.

"In fabric made from a rainbow," Oochigeaskw answered.

"And of what are his moccasins made?"

"His moccasins are made from strips cut from the summer sky."

"And what does he wear upon his head?"

"A cap made from pieces of the sun and pieces of the

moon put together."

"And what does he carry in his hand?"

"He carries a thunderbolt in his hand."

By this time the boy was standing before them.

"Ah, my sister, I see I am discovered," he smiled. And laid down the thunderbolt and reached out and took Oochigeaskw's hand in his.

So she who had been known as She Who Is Covered With Scars became the bride of the invisible boy.

And what happened to the bride's sisters?

Well, there are those who claim they beat one another to death. But it is generally maintained that the sister of the invisible boy turned one into a mosquito and the other into a blackfly. But if such a transformation occured you must not think it was done for revenge. In their new bodies the sisters went on doing exactly what they had done in their old bodies. And, in any case, who among us is bold enough to argue that the race of flies is unhappier than the race of men?

THE CAPTIVE

In the days of the people who are gone, a war party of the enemy fell upon a certain village and killed all its inhabitants except a woman and her baby, whom they made captive and took with them when they went back to their own country, far away in the west.

There, a chief took the woman as his wife, taught her his language and treated her baby as his own son.

Time passed. The woman became accustomed to her new home. The baby grew big enough to play with the other children of the village.

One day when he was about five years old the boy became involved in a quarrel with another boy slightly older than himself.

Suddenly, he was amazed to hear himself being berated as a foreigner and an enemy.

"The man you call your father is not your father!" his antagonist shouted. "I have heard my parents talk of how that man killed your father and brought you and your mother as captives from the land where the sun rises. You do not belong here! You are a miserable slave who should have been tortured to death!"

The little boy was so astonished that he could think of nothing to say. He ran home and asked his mother if what he had been told was true.

"No, it is not true," his mother assured him. "He told those lies because he was angry and wanted to hurt you."

For that moment, the boy was satisfied. But as the years passed, other quarrelsome boys made the same accusation and, from time to time, he overheard his mother say things that indicated she had once lived in another country.

When he was about seventeen, he went to his mother and insisted that she tell him the truth.

"Are you not happy here?" she asked him. "Does your father show you less kindness than other men show their sons?"

"But is this truly my country?" the boy persisted.

"It is the only country you have known," said his mother. "Is that not enough?"

"And is this man really my father?"

"He has treated you as well as your own father could have treated you."

Now the boy was hot on the scent and not to be put off.

"Then you admit he is not my real father!" he cried triumphantly.

His mother saw it was no use to continue her deception. She told him about the husband of her youth, the attack of the war party, the slaughter of all except herself and her baby, her marriage to his foster-father and how she expected that both she and he would end their days here, far from their native place.

"I will not die here," vowed the boy. "I will return to the land of my own people."

Although his mother pleaded with him to forget all that she had been forced to tell him, he insisted that she teach him the language spoken in the land of the Rising Sun. This she agreed to do, provided it was kept a secret between them.

Within a few months, he acquired the language of his ancestors and learned how they lived and who were their gods. And each day he became more contemptuous of the people among whom he lived and more eager to return to the land of his birth.

One night in the dead of winter he stole into the wigwams of the seven greatest warriors in the village and killed them with his tomahawk while they slept.

Then he returned to his own wigwam and killed the chief, his foster-father, strapped on his snowshoes and escaped into the night.

By the time the villagers realized what had happened and organized a war party to pursue the fugitive, it was daybreak. But the boy had not travelled far during the night for fear of getting lost. It was not long before his pursuers found the fresh prints of his snowshoes.

"Soon," they told one another, "we will find the traitor and when we find him he will die such a death as no man before him has ever died!"

But it was not to be, for the boy was both swift and cunning.

Once, when the enemy was almost upon him, he burrowed down into the snow, and though they suspected his ruse and tramped around in circles, driving their spears into the snow near him, they did not find him.

Another time, so it is said, he covered a great distance by leaping from tree to tree like a squirrel, so that he left no tracks.

After several days, the war party gave up the chase and went back to the village.

There, they exacted their vengeance upon the boy's mother — killing her because they believed her to be an accomplice to the deeds of her son.

For weeks, the fugitive travelled toward the rising sun. Often he was hungry. Always he was cold. But he was determined to reach the land of his forefathers.

"When I arrive there," he told himself, "I will be recognized as a great warrior. Perhaps they will even make me a chief, and perhaps one day I will go back with many warriors and destroy all the villages of the people of the west."

The day came when he heard the voices of men speaking in the language of his fathers which his mother had taught him.

With a shout of joy, he ran out of the woods to greet his kinsmen.

The members of the hunting party, for such it was, stared at him in astonishment. They were about a dozen men, armed with spears and bows.

"I am your brother," said the boy, "your brother who was taken prisoner to the land of the enemy. I have escaped and come home to you."

"He speaks our tongue," said one of the hunters, "though he wears the costume of the enemy. Perhaps what he says is true."

"It is our tongue," said another, "but he speaks it strangely. I believe he has been sent by the enemy to spy on us."

"No, no," cried the boy. "I am your brother, one of your people."

He related the story of his capture as he had learned it from his mother and told them how he had made his escape.

The hunters were still convinced that he was a member of a war party sent to attack their village.

"Look at his snowshoes!" cried one. "Only the enemy make snowshoes of that design."

"Look at his weapons!" cried another. "Such weapons are carried only by the warriors from the west."

"He is a spy!" they chorussed. "We must not let him escape!"

The boy was so confused that he began arguing with them in the language of the west. As they gathered around him, shouting and brandishing their spears, he reached for his tomahawk — but it was too late.

Before his hand reached his belt, a spear pierced his body. When he fell, other hunters drove their spears into his chest or struck him with their tomahawks to make sure that he was dead.

"There," they said as they left him. "That should teach those foreign devils not so send their spies into the land of the rising sun."

THE SNOW VAMPIRE

In the days of the people who are gone, a certain young man determined to make the most beautiful girl in his village his wife.

First, as was then the custom, he sent his mother to the wigwam in which the girl lived with her parents to tell them, in the formal manner, that he was tired of living alone.

But when the mother returned from her visit she had to tell the young man that the girl and her parents had rejected his suit.

"They have heard," she told him, "that you are one of those who talk with the dark gods and work with potions and spells. It is their wish that their daughter marry a hunter and warrior. They say they could not sleep at night if they had a wizard for a son-in-law."

"Then I shall talk with the girl herself," said the young man who, in truth, was a magician and, as such, somewhat feared by the inhabitants of his village.

So the following day the young man went straight to the girl and told her he wished to marry her.

"You have no cause to fear me," he said. "True, I talk with the dark gods. But if you become my wife you can be sure I will never use my powers to harm you or your parents. I will adorn my bride with all manner of strange and beautiful things; and her children will learn to fly like hawks in the night."

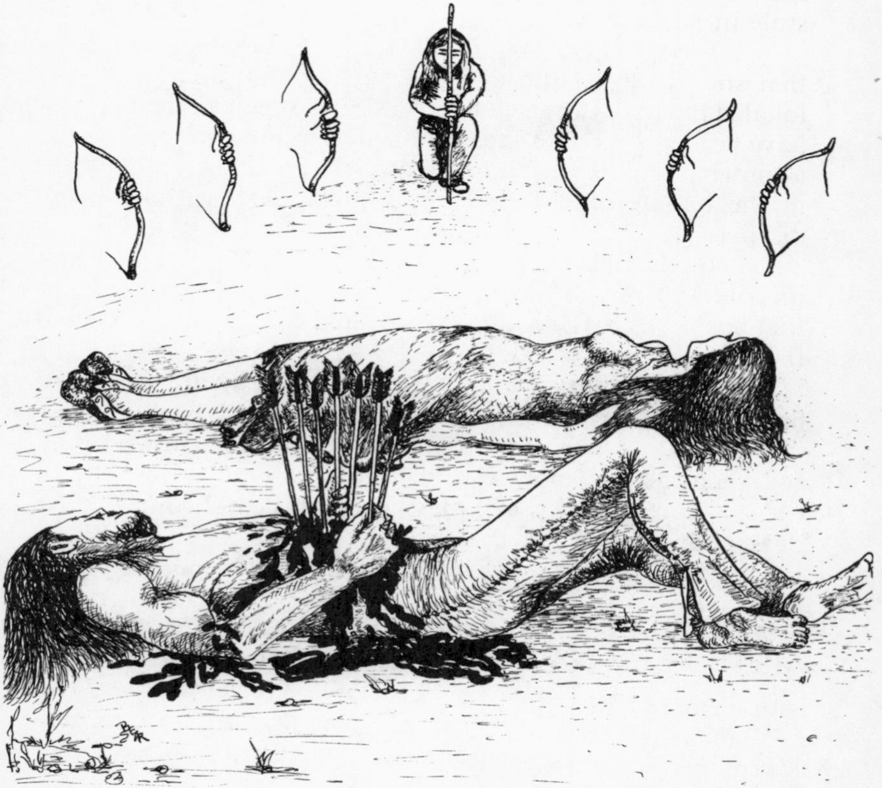

But his words only frightened the girl more. With a cry of terror she ran away and hid from him.

Now that he had been twice rejected — first by the girl's parents and then by the girl herself — the young magician discovered he hated the girl as intensely as, formerly, he had desired her.

"They have been afraid of me without reason," he said to himself. "Now I will give them good reason for fear."

Being a magician, the young man kept many powerful herbs in a medicine bag hidden in his wigwam. One winter's night, not long after the girl had run away and hid from him, the young man took one of the strongest of these herbs and stole into the wigwam where the girl lay sleeping.

First, he held a handful of the herb over the girl's face so that she inhaled it through her nostrils and mouth. As she inhaled the herb the girl fell into a sleep so deep it might almost have been mistaken for death. Then he went outside and made a snowball as large as his two fists. After placing the snowball in the hallow of her neck, he slipped away without being discovered.

By the time the girl awoke the snowball had melted, and its cold had spread through her body, into her very vitals, so that her teeth chattered and she shivered violently from head to foot and would not eat.

Her parents were at a loss to imagine what had happened to her. And their astonishment and fear increased when they saw her go outside the wigwam, get down on all fours and gobble snow as a bear gobbles blueberries.

"Surely, this is evil magic!" cried the old couple. "The dark gods are at work here!"

They remembered how they had offended the young magician.

"What fools we were!" exclaimed the mother. "Better a wizard as a son-in-law than a snow vampire for a daughter!"

For they had begun to realize what had happened to their daughter. In the days of the people who are gone, men and beasts shared the land with creatures that were neither man nor beast. Among these was the snow vampire, the creature of the north, that ate the flesh of men and sometimes even of its own flesh.

Suddenly, the girl left off eating snow and spoke to her parents.

"Yes," she said, "I am changing into a snow vampire and you must kill me before I kill you."

"Kill you?" cried the father, "I'd give up my own life before I'd do such a thing. Snow vampire or not, you are my daughter. If it is our fate to be killed by you we must be prepared to die."

The girl pleaded with her father.

"If you love me, you must kill me," she said. "Only if you hate me can you let me live."

Still he would not do as she asked and the girl wept in despair — for though all snow vampires wish to die it is not possible for such a creature to kill itself.

Each day that followed the girl acquired more of the features and characteristics of the creature of the north. Her parents tied her hands and feet, but she broke the moosehide thongs as though they were thread. There was no controlling her. At times she burst out of the wigwam and chased children like a ravenous wolf. Soon her condition was common knowledge in the village. The day came when the chief and a party of warriors came to demand that she be put to death.

"You cannot kill her!" exclaimed the parents.

But the girl told them to be silent and came forward to address the chief.

"You are quite right," she told him. "For the good of the people, I must be killed. But there is only one way in which it may be possible for you to kill me."

"And how is that?" asked the chief.

"Let seven warriors shoot seven arrows into my body," replied the girl. "Then I may die. But if the arrows do not kill me, be prepared to flee — for if you cannot kill me I will kill all of you."

While the parents lamented, the chief bade seven of the best bowmen fix arrows to their bows.

All these bowmen were saddened by the thing that had to be done. In happier times, several of them had wished to become the husband of the girl. Yet none hesitated to do as he had been told. Each took careful aim and loosed his shaft — and seven arrows sank into the body of the snow vampire.

Now a very strange thing happened. As the life drained from the snow vampire's body, its face, which had been more horrible than that of a man-eating giant, became once again the face of a beautiful young girl.

From this sign, the people knew the snow vampire was truly dead; for had it retained the features of a vampire even in death it could have revived and preyed upon the people.

What was still more strange, the arrows had disappeared and the wounds inflicted by the arrows had vanished so that the girl looked like one who had died peacefully in her sleep.

"Now," said the chief grimly, "we must go and kill the wizard who is to blame for this evil thing."

But when the chief and his warriors came near the wigwam of the young magician they heard his mother singing the death song of her clan.

And when they went inside they found the body of the young man lying upon the ground with seven arrows planted in its heart.

THE CHIEF WHO REFUSED TO DIE

In the days of the people who are gone, there lived a great war chief named Ulgimmo. Ten times he drove the enemy out of the Land of the Rising Sun and sent him fleeing back to his home in the west.

He was one of the greatest archers who ever lived. His spear always found its target. None excelled him in the use of the knife and the tomahawk. Moreover, he was one of those who talked with the dark gods: his skill in magic enabled him to live to be one hundred and three years old.

When Ulgimmo was already very old his god, Otter, warned him that a raiding party was approaching his village from the north. But Ulgimmo told the young men that the danger lay in the west, so that they went off in the wrong direction, leaving the old men, women and children behind, where they believed they would be safe.

When the enemy warriors entered the village, Ulgimmo went forth to meet them. He was bent and lame and the young warriors thrust him aside contemptuously.

"Get out of our way, old fool!" they shouted. "You are not worth killing and would be useless as a slave. Go into your wigwam and thank your gods that it was our whim to let you live."

But one of the older raiders recognized Ulgimmo, seized him and dragged him before the chief.

"I know this man," he cried. "It is Ulgimmo, one of those who have waded in our people's blood."

"Can this be?" wondered the chief. "I have heard my grandfather tell how his grandfather did battle with Ulgimmo and died by his hand. If the man still lives he must be older than the trees."

The prisoner raised himself to his full height. "I am Ulgimmo who killed the grandfather of your grandfather," said he.

Soon a great many warriors gathered around the old man and stared at him with eyes in which hatred mingled with awe. Truth to tell, they were a little afraid of him, despite his age and infirmities, for they had heard legends of his prowess and many of them knew, also, that he was a great magician.

On one thing they were agreed: he must die. The only question was how he could best be put to death. Some clamoured for the death of knives and some for the death of fire.

While the raiders argued how they should kill Ulgimmo the inhabitants of the village escaped, one by one, into the surrounding forest.

It was finally decided that the old man should die the death of fire. Under the blows and kicks of the raiders, Ulgimmo was made to gather wood for his own funeral pyre.

"And mind that it is not too dry," said the chief, "for we would not wish this old one's death to come too soon."

When the chief was satisfied that enough fuel had been gathered, Ulgimmo was bound to a stake and the wood piled around him. A torch was put to the pile and the flames rose around the old man's body.

As the fire enveloped Ulgimmo, the raiders danced around him, chanting their war songs and brandishing their tomahawks.

So caught up were they in their triumph and mockery that they did not notice that their victim was not singing his death song. Instead, he was whispering with his dark god, Otter.

They were frozen with fear and amazement when Ulgimmo burst free of his bonds and sprung from the midst of the fire.

Suddenly, he was no longer ancient and stooped but young and straight as an arrow. Snatching a tomahawk from the man nearest him, he lay about him to left and to right. Warriors fell under his hand like rabbits.

In less time than it takes to tell it, Ulgimmo had killed all but three of the raiders. He himself had not suffered so much as a single scratch. Having marked the faces of the survivors with a knife, he bade them return to their homeland.

"Go tell your people," he said, "that one man from the Land of the Rising Sun, even if he be a hundred years old, is a match for the largest war party they can send from the west."

That night the young men returned from their fruitless quest and the old men, women and children crept back from their hiding places in the woods. The bodies of the fallen raiders lay everywhere, and Ulgimmo was once again a lame old man, leaning on a staff.

At the beginning of the following winter, Ulgimmo died. Before he died, he told his people they must not bury his body but leave it on a high shelf of rock. This they did, then went off to their winter quarters and did not return until the following spring.

When they came back to the place where they had left his body, they expected to find that it had been eaten by animals. The bravest warriors cried out in fear when they saw the old man had come back to life and was walking about.

"Do not be afraid of me," he told them. "You were not afraid of me while I lived. Surely there is less reason for you to fear a dead man than a living one. Come. Let us talk and eat together."

The people reminded one another of the great deeds that had been done in their behalf by Ulgimmo.

"When I was a baby I was taken captive by the people of the west," said one, "and Ulgimmo killed my captors and brought me back to my parents."

"He saved my life," said another, "when I was ambushed by the enemy."

"Often," said an old woman, "there was no food in my wigwam and Ulgimmo came with gifts of rich meat."

"There is not a person in our village who is not indebted to Ulgimmo," they agreed. "But he has talked too much with the dark gods. It is not possible he will bring them to fall upon us in our sleep?"

The people could not shake off their fear of the man who had died and come back to life.

That summer, Ulgimmo behaved no differently than he had ever done. By day, he hobbled about the village, leaning heavily on his staff; by night, so it was said, he went into the forest and talked with Otter.

"We have nothing to fear from the men of the west so long as Ulgimmo lives," some of the villagers said. "By his magic he can transform himself from an old man into a young warrior, as he did when the enemy last attacked us."

"Perhaps," said others, "but who is to say that Ulgimmo's magic is not more to be feared than the arrows and tomahawks of the enemy."

Fall came, and Ulgimmo told the people that he must die again. This time, he said, they must bury him but after one night they must open the grave and he would come out and remain with them forever. He gave them a sign by which they would know when to open the grave. The day would be clear, without a single cloud to be seen, but out of the sky would come a peel of thunder. At that moment, he said, they must open his grave.

"Yes, yes," chorused the people. "It shall be done and you shall stay with us and protect us for ever."

The next day, Ulgimmo died. The villagers dug his grave very deep and, when they had refilled it, piled a great mound of stones atop it. When the peel of thunder came from the clear sky the village was deserted and Ulgimmo's people were far away.

BROTHER TO THE BEARS

In the days of the people who are gone, there lived a small boy whose parents were dead. Having no home of his own, he lived sometimes in one wigwam and sometimes in another.

Because the lonely find their loneliness easier to bear when they are alone, he often went off by himself into the forest.

One fall day, after spending an afternoon in the woods, he discovered that he was lost. Night began to fall. Try as he might, he could not find his way back to the village. Darkness came. Still he attempted to retrace his steps.

After walking a great distance, he saw the light of a wigwam. As he came closer, he heard persons talking together.

Of course, he had no way of knowing what sort of people lived there. But he was too tired, cold and hungry to be much afraid. After hesitating only a moment, he went up to the wigwam and lifted the door blanket.

Imagine his astonishment when he saw not man but bears — an old she-bear and her two cubs — eating and talking together!

He would have run away, but the old bear beckoned for him to enter and the cubs pointed at his face and laughed so hard he could not believe he had any cause to fear them.

Moreover, the old bear gestured for him to take a seat near the fire, and handed him dried meat and a birchen vessel full of berries.

"Surely, this is a dream," he thought. "I have fallen asleep in the woods. In the morning, when I awake, I'll return to my village. But, in the meantime, these animals cannot hurt me — for, after all, this is only a dream."

So he ate greedily of meat and berries and after he had eaten he, in truth, fell asleep.

When he awoke, he found that it was spring.

He had slept all winter in the den of the bears, although he felt no different than if he had slept a single night.

His first though was: "I must hasten back to my village. I have been gone so long my people will have given me up for dead."

But then, he reflected: "Who is there to care whether or not I return? I am an orphan. The people fed me only from pity. They will be happier if I do not go back to them."

So he decided to stay with the bears as long as they would have him.

And he found, to his amazement and delight, that the old bear treated him exactly as she treated her sons, and the cubs treated him like a brother.

Soon, by listening carefully, he learned the language of the bears so that he could converse with them. The cubs taught him the games that are played by the young of the bear people. And they went fishing for smelts, the four of them, the three youngsters wading in the water and driving the fish toward the mother, who scooped them up with her paws and threw them on the riverbank, in the manner of bears.

The cubs were so young that the boy was their equal in strength and delighted in wrestling with them. The old bear, who was famous among her people for her wisdom, revealed to the boy many of the secrets of the forest that have been hidden from men.

Never had the boy been so happy. For now he had a family of his own.

Sometimes men passed through that part of the woods. Then he and the cubs would hide behind the old bear who would stand guard, sniffing the air, until long after the men disappeared from sight.

"If men see us they will attempt to kill us," she told

them. "If they make such an attempt, I will attack them. That will give you time to run away and hide where they cannot find you."

"When I grow up, I will gather together all the bears in the world and make war upon men," vowed the boy.

The cubs only laughed at him.

"Listen to the braggart," scoffed the smallest of the cubs. "Only this morning I beat him at wrestling; yet now he is ready to make war upon the whole race of men."

But the old bear did not laugh.

"Ah, my poor little one," she said, "you do not know what you are saying. Do not forget that you yourself belong to the people called men."

The boy almost wept.

"Don't say that!" he pleaded. "I am not a man, but a bear. You are my mother, and these are my brothers."

"We shall see. We shall see," said the old bear.

The boy wished so much to belong to the bear people that sometimes he imagined that long black hairs were beginning to sprout from his human flesh. Often, when he was alone, he stared at his hands until he almost believed that they were growing into paws strong enough to break a man's neck with a single blow. And he knelt by the river and stared at the reflection of his face, trying to convince himself that it was becoming more and more the face of a bear.

"I am a bear," he told the cubs. "A bear like you."

"Yes, yes," they assured him, "you are a bear."

But as time passed he came to seek this reassurance so often that they began to weary of it.

Besides, as the cubs grew they became so much stronger than he that he no longer wrestled with them. The old bear sometimes cuffed them for being too rough with him. And, of course, they were much quicker than he in learning the skills that must be acquired by all young bears. As fall approached again, they could snatch fish from the river almost as rapidly as their mother. The boy seldom managed to grab a fish and when he did it usually slipped out of his hand.

One day, when he had lived with the bears for almost a year, the old bear called him aside.

"Little one," she said, "you know that I love you as I love my own sons."

The boy threw his arms around her.

"Oh, yes, yes!" he cried. "And I love you as much as I could have loved my own mother, had I ever known her."

"I want you to know that it is because I love you that I am sending you away," said the old bear.

"Sending me away!" cried the boy. "Where will I go?"

"You will go back to your own people," said the old bear.

"But I am of the bear people!" said the boy.

"Do not talk nonsense, little one," said the old bear. "Do you wear the skin of a bear? Are your hands a bear's paw? Is your face the face of a bear? No, you are a man and your place is with the race of men."

The boy pleaded with her, but the old bear was not to be gainsayed.

"If you stay here," she told him, "you will grow up to be the weakest and clumsiest bear in the forest. Other bears will scorn you. You will do well to feed yourself. Your sense of smell is so weak that you will never be able to detect the presence of the hunters in time to escape their shafts. And the hunter who kills you will not even bother to skin you — of what use would be your pelt? He will leave your carcass for the scavangers. But if you go back to the world of men, you will become one of the greatest hunters and warriors in the world."

So the boy said goodbye to the old bear and the cubs and went back through the forest to his village, where the people had long ago decided that he was dead.

When he grew up, it was as the old bear had predicted: he became a great warrior and hunter, of whom songs were sung and stories told by the campfires. And he taught his children the language of the bears, and his children taught their children, so that his descendants can converse with bears to this very day.

THE MAN WHO WANTED TO LIVE FOR EVER

In the days of the people who are gone, when Glooskap still lived among men, there was a man who was sick with the fear of death.

None wailed louder than he when death visited his village, for always when he looked upon the dead he saw his own face.

Yet he was brave in war and killed many of the enemy — partly because he was ashamed of his great fear and partly because he half-believed that the lives of those he killed would be added to his. Perhaps, thought he, if I kill enough men I will never die!

But when he reflected that the greatest warriors died as soon as other men, and often sooner, he knew his dream was foolish, and his despair became greater than before.

In his hunger for knowledge as to how he might escape death, he questioned the oldest man in his village, one so old he looked as if he might have lived since the creation of the world.

"Grandfather," he said, "is it true that you possess the secret of life? If so, tell me and name your own reward for I, too, would conquer death."

The toothless old man laughed.

"Poor foolish one," he said, "man's life is as from sunrise to sunset. When I look back over my life it seems I have lived no longer than a butterfly. Perhaps I shall die this

very night. I doubt that even Glooskap himself will cheat death."

"Glooskap," cried the younger man. "Why did I not think of that before? He has lived since there were first men in this land. I will go to him in search of that which will enable me to live forever!"

And he ran off, leaving the old man laughing at the door of his wigwam.

Now, in those days it was not difficult to find Glooskap, for this was before he left his people and went to his secret home in the west.

Seven days' journey from his village, the man who was afraid of death came to the mountain where Glooskap lived with his mother, Grandmother Bear, and his younger brother, Little Marten. And when the man came to Glooskap's wigwam he went in and ate with them.

How astonished he was to see that though Grandmother Bear put nothing but a single, fleshless bone in the pot, the soup was as rich as that made from the fattest meat! And though all four ate as much as they desired, the pot remained full.

When they had finished eating, the man sought to discuss the purpose of his visit with Glooskap.

"Is it true," he asked, "that you give men all that they ask of you?"

Glooskap smiled. "There are many men and they ask many things of me," he said. "I give them what I can. What is it you wish me to give to you?"

"Life!" cried the man. "A life that will never end!"

Grandmother Bear chuckled. Little Marten hid his smile with his hands. "I am glad, my brother, that these humans are your friends and not mine," Little Marten said. "My people ask only for food and relief from pain. Humans would not rest content if you made them higher than the gods."

"Hush, little brother," said Glooskap. "Would you insult our guest?" He turned back to the man. "Alas, my friend, not even a god can give you what he does not possess. Even I will die. Even my little brother. Yes, even our mother will go down to death. Perhaps, when all else is dead, even death will die. This being so, how can one as small and powerless as you dare even think of cheating death?"

But the man persisted.

"Perhaps," he said, "you cannot give me the eternal life I desire. But surely you have the power to lengthen life. I beg of you to lengthen mine!"

And the man fell at the feet of the god.

Glooskap frowned. "Yes," he admitted, "I can make you live longer than any of your race has ever lived. But are you certain that is what you want?"

"Yes, yes, yes!" cried the man. "Give me what I ask and I will sing your praises until I die!"

"Then so be it," said Glooskap. "But I warn you that men have cursed me because I satisfied their desires."

So the next morning, after they had again eaten from the pot which is never empty, Glooskap took the man into his canoe and paddled across the great waters to an island which could scarcely be seen from the mainland. The island was so rocky that neither men nor animals lived there, but the man scarcely noticed this, so obsessed was he with his hunger for life.

As soon as they went ashore, Glooskap clasped the man around the legs, lifted him from the ground and put him down again.

"There," said he, "I have granted you your wish!" And when the man looked down he saw that he had been changed into a cedar tree — an old gnarled tree with many rough and ugly branches. He was too astonished to speak.

"I cannot tell exactly how long you will live," said Glooskap. "Only the father of gods and men can tell that. But I don't think you're likely to be disturbed for a good, long while, as no man could have any reason for cutting you down, and you are strong enough to withstand my brothers, the wind god and the god of the sea, though I doubt they will think it worthwhile to ever much trouble you."

Glooskap climbed back into his canoe and paddled away from the island, meditating on the folly of man. And the cedar tree that had been a man stared after him until he disappeared from sight.